CONTENTS

GW01003500

N

O

P

Q

R

S

T

U

V

W

X

Y

Z

A

A few sandwiches short of a picnic – A stupid person.

A few stubbies short of a six-pack – A stupid person.

Acca Dacca - It is a term of endearment for the Australian hard rock group called AC/DC.

Ace! - (1) Excellent! (2) Great!

acker – A pimple.

ACT - It is an acronym for Australian Capital City.

act the angora - Behaving foolishly or in a silly manner.

act the goat - Behaving foolishly or in a silly manner. *e.g.* *'Stop acting the goat in this classroom!'*

add fuel to the fire - To make a bad situation worse.

Advance Australia Fair - It is the national anthem of Australia.

aero ping-pong – It is a derogatory term used to refer to the sport Australian Rules Football.

aerogard - Any insect repellent.

AFL - It is an acronym for Australian Football League.

after darks - It is a rhyming slang meaning sharks.

aggro - It is an abbreviation for aggressive. *e.g.* *'Don't be so aggro!'*

aggy pile - It is short for Agricultural pipe.

airhead - A brainless person.

airy-fairy - (1) Absent-minded. (2) It is used to describe something being of very little practical value or significance. (3) Vague.

Akubra - An Australian brand of a wide-brimmed hat that is made of felted rabbit fur and this kind of hat are used by farmers and country dwellers for protection from the sun and weather. *e.g.* *'He wore his stylish Akubra and headed to a pub for some amber fluid.'*

Al Capone - It is a rhyming slang meaning telephone.

Al desko - Eating lunch at one's desk while working.

alf - An uncultivated Australian.

alfoil - Aluminium foil.

alkie - An alcoholic. *e.g.* *'That funny looking bloke is an alkie.'*

all alone like a country dunny – On your own.

All Blacks - The New Zealand national rugby union team.

all froth and no beer - No substance.

all in – Very tired.

all over red rover - Something that has been completed or finished.

all over the place like a mad woman's breakfast – A total mess.

all the go – Popular.

all to smash – To be ruined.

all wet - (1) Completely wrong. (2) Foolish. (3) Ridiculous.

all wind and water - A person who just talks about doing something but never does it.

amber fluid - Beer.

amber nectar - Beer.

ambo - (1) It is short for an ambulance. (2) It is a member of an ambulance crew.

ammo - It is short for ammunition.

anchors – Car brakes.

ankle-biter - A small or a young child. *'This is me ankie-biter.'*

ano - It is an abbreviation for anorexic.

anothery - Another one. *e.g. 'His sis Mary is expecting anothery in January next year.'*

answer is lemon – A meaningless reply.

any tick of the clock - Very soon.

ANZAC – (1) It stands for Australian and New Zealand Army Corps. (2) A member of the Australian and New Zealand Army Corps.

Apple eater - Someone who comes from Tasmania in which apples are grown widely.

Apple Island - Tasmania.

Apple Isle - Tasmania.

apples - All right. *e.g. 'She'll be apples mate!'*

apples and pears - It is a rhyming slang meaning stairs.

apple sauce - It is a rhyming slang meaning horse.

argie-bargie - A heated argument or general unrest.*e.g. 'I have seen two blokes engaging in some argie-bargie outside the pub.'*

argue the toss - To continue a dispute over a final decision that has been made or after a matter has been settled. *e.g. 'There is no point in arguing the toss with the umpire.'*

around the twist - Insane.

Aristotle - It is a rhyming slang meaning bottle, that is usually filled up with beer.

around the traps - (1) A regular visiting place. (2) Around the area. (3) Out and about.

arvo - It is an abbreviation for afternoon. *e.g.* *'Shall we go to the shops this arvo?'*

as easy as spearing an eel with a spoon – Extremely difficult.

as if! – It is a mocking interjection used to express complete disbelief or disagreement.

as slow as a wet week – Very slow.

as the crow flies – A direct route.

as useful as lips on a chicken – Someone or something is useless.

Athens of the south - Melbourne, which is the state capital of Victoria.

Aussie - Australian.

Aussieland - Australia.

Aussie battler - An ordinary Australian trying to have enough money to live on.

Aussie Rules - Australian Rules Football.

Aussie salute - Flapping one's hand in front of the face to get rid of the flies.

Australian as a kangaroo - Genuinely Australian.

Australian as a meat pie - Truly Australian.

avo - It is an abbreviation for Avocado.

away with the pixies - Dreaming.

awning over the toy shop – The beer belly of a man.

axle grease - (1) Butter. (2) Money. (3) Vegemite.

B

babbling brook - It is a rhyming slang for a cook.

baccy – Tobacco.

back-hander – A bribe.

backblocks – Outside suburbia.

backseat bogan – It is a person who sits at the back of the bus.

backside – One's behind.

bad news – It is a person who is causing difficulty or annoyance to others.

baggy green – It is a dark myrtle green cricket cap that is worn by Australian Test Cricketers.

bail out – To depart.

bald as a bandicoot – Remarkably bald.

ball of muscle – A person who is very healthy, contented and having a good time.

ball-tearer – It is something astonishing, brilliant or thrilling.

banana bender - A person who resides in Queensland.

Bananaland - Queensland.

bang in the middle – Exactly in the middle.

banged up - Pregnant.

banger - Australian sausage.

banjo – A shovel.

barbed wire – It is another name for the Castlemaine XXXX beer, a popular. Queensland beer. It is called this because the logo on the beer bottle being four X resembles a barbed wine.

barbie – A barbecue. *'Today is a perfect day to have a **barbie** with me mates.'*

barf – To vomit.*e.g.* *'I think he's gonna **barf** at any moment.'*

bark at the lawn – To vomit.

Barker's eggs – The excrements of a dog. *e.g.* *'He just trod on some **Barker's eggs**.'*

barmy as a bandicoot – Insane.

barney – An argument or a fight.

Barra – A Barramundi fish.*e.g.* *'I have caught a few **Barra** on today.'*

barrack – To cheer loudly, usually for ones favourite sport's team.

barrel of fat - It is a rhyming slang for hat.

Barry Crocker – It is a rhyming slang for shocker.

bathers – A swimming costume.

BBQ – A barbecue.

bean counter – An accountant.

beanie – It is a hat that is tight-fitting and is usually wholly or partly made of wool.

beat it – (1) Go away! (2) Leave.

beaut! – It is an interjection of one's approval, delight, enthusiasm or satisfaction towards something or someone.

beauty! – It is an interjection of one's approval, delight, enthusiasm or satisfaction towards something or someone.

beer gut - It is a man's large or protruding belly is due to excessive consumption of beer.

Beer o'clock - It is the time to start having a beer.

bee's knees – (1) Really great. (2) The best.

beg yours? – (1) Excuse me?. (2) I beg your pardon? (3) Would you mind repeating that?

bell – (1) A telephone call. (2) To give someone a call on the telephone. *e.g.* *'I'll **bell** you this arvo.'*

belt up! – It is a command to tell someone to be quiet or to stop talking.*e.g.* *'I don't understand why he doesn't **belt up**.'*

bend the elbow – Drinking a beer.

bender – (1) A heavy drinking session. (2) A wild drinking spree.

berk – An idiot.

berley – It is any materials making up the bait that is added to the water and spread over the water to attract the fish during fishing.

berko – Being out of control with anger or excitement.

Betcha! – It is a contracted form of bet you.

better than a poke in the eye with a burnt stick – Better than nothing.

bewdy! – It is an exclamation of one's approval, delight, enthusiasm or satisfaction towards something or someone.

bib and bub – A tub.

bib and tucker – Clothes.

biccy - It is short for biscuit.

biffo - (1) An argument. (2) A brawl.

big ask - (1) A huge favour. (2) A request that is not easy to achieve.

big bickies – A lot of money.

big smoke – (1) A big town. (2) A city.

big spit – To vomit.

big sticks – These are the centre goal posts used in Australian Rules Football.

bikkie – A biscuit.

billabong – A waterhole.

billy – It is a tin can that is used for brewing tea, boiling water and cooking over a campfire.

billy bluegum – A koala bear.

billy lids – It is a rhyming slang meaning kids. *e.g.* *'These are me billy lids.'*

billyo – At a fast speed.

binge – A drinking spree.

bingle – A minor vehicle accident.

bizzo - It is an abbreviation for business. *e.g.* *'Please mind your own bizzo.'*

blimey! – An expression of surprise or wonder.

blind as a welders dog – To be extremely drunk.

blithered – Foolishly drunk.

bloke – A male person.

blood blister - A rhyming slang meaning sister.

bloody oath – That is undoubtedly the truth.

bloody ripper – Really awesome.

blotto – Incredibly drunk.

blowie – A blowfly.

blow in the bag – Have a breathalyser test.

blow a blue dog off its chain – Extremely windy.

bludger – A lazy or idle person.

Blue Heeler – (1) A member of the police force. (2) It is a breed of Australian Cattle dog that handles herds of cattle on an expansive ranch by nipping their heels.

BO – It is an acronym for body odour. *e.g.* *'That bloke got the worst BO ever.'*

bo peep - It is a rhyming slang for sleep.

boardies – These are surfers' boardshorts.

boat race - It is a rhyming slang for face.

bog in – Participate in something with enjoyment and enthusiasm.

bodgy - (1) Fake. (2) Inferior. (3) Poorly made. (4) Worthless.

bombed out - (1) Drunk. (2) Unsuccessful.

bonehead – A stupid person.

bonza! – Excellent!

bonzer! – Excellent! *e.g.* *'That musical performance was **bonzer!**'*

boofhead - (1) A foolish person. (2) Someone who has a big head.

boogie board – A half-sized surfboard.

boomer – A large kangaroo.

bookie – A bookmaker.

boot – It is the trunk of an automobile.

booze – Alcohol.

booze artist – It is a person who drinks habitually and usually gets drunk afterwards.

booze bus – It is a police vehicle used for alcohol testing of drivers and catching drunk drivers.

bosker - (1) Excellent. (2) Good.

Bottle-o – A liquor store.

bottle shop – A liquor store.

bottoms up! – Cheers! It is an interjection used when drinking with other people.

boys in blue – The police officers.

brasco – A toilet.

brass monkey weather – very cold weather.

bread and jam - It is a rhyming slang for tram.

break open a coldie - To open a can of beer.

brekkie - Breakfast.

brew – (1) A beverage. (2) A cup or pot of tea or coffee.

brick venereal - It is a derogatory term for a brick-veneer house or any property in a housing development with a similar design to a brick-veneer home.

brickie - It is an abbreviation for a Bricklayer.

Brisbanite - One who comes from Brisbane.

Brissie - Brisbane.

brolly – An umbrella.

Brumby – A wild horse.

bub – (1) Baby. (2) It is a term of endearment for the girlfriend, a wife, a woman, etc.

bubbler – A drinking fountain.

buck up! – It is a way of asking someone to become more cheerful or more positive.

Buckley's chance – A low possibility that something will happen.

bugger around - (1) Behave foolishly. (2) Fiddle around. (3) Mess around.

buggered- (1) Broken. (2) Ruined. (3) Very tired.

bull dust – (1) A lie. (2) Nonsense.

bung - (1) Broken. (2) Pretend. (3) Put or place it down carelessly.

bush ballad – It is a kind of poem or folk music that portrays the life, the characters and the scenery of the Australian bush.

bush chook – An emu.

bush telegraph - It is the informal network that passes gossip and news through outback Australia or a region of rural.

bush tucker - (1) It is any native Australian animal or plant found in the bush and used traditionally as food by the Aboriginal Australians for their nourishment. (2) It is any native fauna or flora found in the bush and used for culinary or medicinal purposes or both.

bushie – It is a person who lives in a bush.

bushman's alarm – A kookaburra.

bushman's clock – A kookaburra.

bushman's handkerchief – It is an act of clearing one's nose by pushing one nostril down with the forefinger finger while blowing the nasal mucus out from the opened nostril to the ground.

bush telly - (1) A campfire. (2) Gazing at the stars in the night sky during camping in the bush is for entertainment.

bushwhacked – Extremely tired.

Bushwhacker – A person who lives in the bush.

Butcher's hook - It is a rhyming slang for look.

BYO – It is an acronym for bring your own. It is an Australian custom for diners to bring their alcohol to a restaurant that does not hold a liquor license.

C

cabbage patcher – A Victorian.

Cabbie – A Taxi driver.

cack handed – (1) Clumsy. (2) Left-handed.

cack oneself – To laugh uncontrollably.

cackle berry – A hen's egg that is used for food. *e.g.* *'She loves to eat a boiled **cackle berry** and a bowl of oats every day for brekkie.*

cactus – It is used to describe something that is not working or useless.

cakehole – A person's mouth. This slang word is considered as mildly offensive by many people. *e.g.* *'Shut your **cakehole**!'*

cancer stick – A cigarette.

canoes - It is a rhyming slang for shoes.

Captain Cook - It is a rhyming slang meaning to take a look. *e.g.* *'Let's have a **Captain Cook** around this place.'*

carby - It is short for a carburettor.

cardie - It is short for Cardigan.

cark it – (1) To break. (2) To die.

carn! – Come on! *e.g.* *'**Carn** the Crows!'*

carry on like a pork chop – To make a fuss or become overreacted over nothing.

carpet grub – A small child.

cashed-up – Having the money available for spending straight away if required.

cattle duffer – A cattle thief.

Caulie - It is short for Cauliflower.

Centralia - The central areas of Australia around Alice Springs.

chalkie – A school teacher.

champers – A champagne.

charge like a wounded bull – To charge or set exorbitant prices.

chatterbox – A talkative person.

cheap as chips – Very low cost.

cheapie – It is something that is low-priced.

cheerio – Goodbye.

cheers – thank you.

cheese and kisses - It is a rhyming slang for missus.

cheese off – Irritated.

cherry plum - It is a rhyming slang for mum.

chew and spew - It is a fast-food outlet.

chew the fat – Have a good talk together.

chewie – Chewing gum.

chiack – To tease.

chicken out – Withdraw oneself from doing something because of cowardice or fear.

chillax – (1) Behave. (2) Calm down. (3) Relax.

china plate - It is a rhyming slang for mate.

chinwag – A conversation.

chippie – A carpenter.

choccy - It is short for Chocolate.

choccy biccy - It is short for Chocolate biscuit.

chockie - It is short for Chocolate.

choke a darkie – Have a bowel movement.

choof off – To leave.

chook – A chicken, usually a hen.

chook house – It is a house or a shed for a chicken.

choom – An Englishman.

chop chop! – It is an interjection demanding someone to hurry up.

chrissie – Christmas.

chrome dome – A person with a bald head.

chuck a sickie – Take time off school or work due to sickness without necessarily feeling ill.

chuck a spaz – To throw a tantrum.

chuck a U-ee – To do a U-Turn in the car.

chuck up – To vomit.

chuck a wobbly – Go crazy.

chucker out – A bouncer.

chuddy – Chewing gum.

chuffed – Very happy.

chunder – To vomit.

chunder loo – It is a rhyming slang for spew.

city of churches – Adelaide.

clackers – False teeth.

clapped out old bomb – (1) It is an automobile that is broken down. (2) It is an automobile that is old and is in poor working conditions.

Clayton's – A substitute for the real thing.

cleanskin – It is a term for cattle that have not been branded, castrated or earmarked.

clear as mud – Confusing.

click – A kilometre. *e.g.* *'He lives a few **clicks** away from me house.'*

close shave – Very close indeed.

clucky – A person who is desirous of having children.

clued-up – Well informed.

cluey – (1) Bright. (2) Knowledgeable.

Coathanger – It is a nickname for the Sydney Harbour Bridge.

cobber – A friend.

codswallop – Nonsense.

coffin nail – A cigarette.

coldie – A can of cold beer.

colourful yawn – Vomit.

combo - It is short for combination.

come off the grass – Just tell me the truth.

come the raw prawn – Try to deceive.

comic cuts - It is a rhyming slang for guts.

compo - Worker's compensation payments.

conk – A nose.

conk out – It is used to describe a machine or an engine that has either broken down or stop working.

convo - It is an abbreviation for conversation.

cooee – It is a word spoken out loudly in the bush to attract attention or to ask for assistance.

coola bin – An esky.

coot – An old unpleasant man.

cop a load of that! – Look at that!

cop – A police officer.

cop shop – A police station.

copper – A police officer.

cossie – A swimming costume.

cot – A bed.

cot case – It is a person who is or should be confined to the bed because he or she is too ill, exhausted or very drunk.

cough potato – It is a person who spends a great deal of time sitting and watching television and doing nothing else.

couldn't organise a chook raffle at a poultry farm - (1) Disorganised. (2) Useless.

couldn't work in an iron lung – It is used to describe a person that is lazy.

counter lunch – A pub lunch.

country cousin - It is a rhyming slang for dozen.

cow cocky – A small-scale cattle farmer.

crack a tinnie – To open a can of beer.

cranky - (1) Angry. (2) Is in a bad mood.

crap - (1) Bad. (2) Terrible.

crapper – It is a vulgar slang for toilet.

crash hot – Marvellous.

crikey! – It is an interjection of astonishment.

crim - It is an abbreviation for criminal.

croc - It is an abbreviation for Crocodile.

crook – (1) Feeling ill or sick. (2) Injured (3) Sore. (4) Suffering from a hangover due to heavy drinking.

crook as chook – Feeling very unwell.

crook as Rookwood - (1) Dying. (2) Very ill.

crooked – Dishonest.

crooked on – Angry with someone.

crow eater - A South Australian.

cuppa – A cup of coffee or tea.

curry and rice - It is a rhyming slang for price.

D

dacks – A pair of pants or trousers.

dad and dave – It is a rhyming slang meaning a shave.

dag – It is a person who either behaves or dresses in an unfashionable way.

damage - (1) The charge. (2) The cost. (3) The expense.

D and M – It is short for Deep and Meaningful, usually referred to the conversation concerning the problems in interpersonal relationships.

darl – It is short for darling.

dart – A cigarette.

Darwinian – A person from Darwin.

date roll – A roll of toilet paper.

David Gower – It is a rhyming slang for shower.

dead centre – The arid central regions of Australia.

dead heart – The arid central regions of Australia.

dead horse – It is a rhyming slang meaning tomato sauce.

dead marine – An empty beer or whisky bottle.

dead ringer – It is either a person or a thing that closely resembles another.

dead-set – Genuine. *e.g.* '*Is that dead-set mate?*'

deep sinker – A long glass of beer.

delish – It is short for delicious.

dekko – A look or a close look. . *e.g.* '*Take a dekko at his house.*'

demo – It is short for demonstration.

dero – It is short for derelict, which means a beggar or a homeless person.

dial – face.

dice – (1) Discard. (2) Throw away.

diddle - (1) Con. (2) Deceive.

Didgeridoo – It is an aboriginal musical instrument made from a hollowed log.

digger – (1) An Australian soldier. (2) A gold miner.

dill – A foolish or a gullible person.

dillpot – A foolish or a gullible person.

dillybag – It is a small carry bag or basket, made from woven fibre or grass, featuring a traditional Aboriginal design on it.

dimwit – A stupid person.

dingbat – An eccentric person or a fool.

Dingo – It is an Australian native dog who has a tawny coat.

dingo's breakfast – No breakfast.

dinki-di – The real thing.

dinkum oil - (1) Good advice. (2) Authentic Information. (3) Confidential information. (4) The truth.

divvy up – (1) To divide up. (2) To share out.

divvy van – A police van.

doco - It is short for documentary.

docket - (1) A bill. (2) A receipt.

dodge and shirk - It is a rhyming slang meaning work.

dodgy - Suspicious.

doer - (1) A hard and keen worker. (2) It is a person who becomes successful through working hard in an honest way.

dog and bone - It is a rhyming slang for phone.

dog's breakfast – It is referred to a person, a situation or a thing, that is messy.*e.g.* *'My kid's room could be described as a **dog's breakfast**.'*

dog's eye - It is a rhyming slang meaning meat pie. *e.g.* *'How to eat a **dog's eye** and dead horse the Aussie way?'*

dole bludger – It is a derisive term for a person who is currently unemployed and fit to work, prefers to live on social security benefits instead of looking for an actual job.

dong – To hit or punch someone.

don't come the raw prawn with me! – Do not try to deceive me or lie to me!

doona – A duvet.

donkey's years – A very long time.

don't get off your bike – Calm down.

dosh – Money.

dover – It is a clasp knife used by a bushman.

down under – (1) Australia.*e.g.* *'Welcome to **down under**!'* (2) Australia and New Zealand.

drack – It is a derogatory term for a person who is dishevelled or unattractive.

drink with the flies – To drink alone.

drippy – Boring.

drive the porcelain bus – Vomit in large amounts into the toilet bowl while holding two hands onto its rim just like holding a steering wheel.

drongo – A foolish or a stupid person. *e.g.* *'I saw a **drongo** driving flat chat down the road like a lunatic.'*

dropkick – An idiot.

drop one's lunch – To break wind.

drunk as a lord – Very drunk.

ducks and geeses - A rhyming slang for police.

duds – (1) A pair of trousers. (2) Clothes, especially ones that are old or worn out.

dunlop cheque – A bounced cheque.

dunny – A toilet. *e.g.* *'I gotta go to the **dunny**.'*

dunny budgie – A big blowfly.

dunny diver – A plumber.

durry – A cigarette.

E

eating irons – A military slang for Cutlery.

egg beater – Helicopter.

egg flip - It is a rhyming slang for tip, which is a tip in horse racing.

eggshell blonde– It is a man who is bald.

earbash – To talk incessantly.

earbasher – A nagger.

Eastralia – Eastern Australia.

easy as spearing an eel with a spoon – Extremely hard.

easy – It is a word to describe a person who is neither worried nor interested concerning the outcome of a particular matter.

easy peasy – Extremely easy.

eau de cologne - It is a rhyming slang meaning Telephone.

el cheapo - Cheap.*e.g.* *'Let's head to the pub for an el cheapo but a tasty meal.'*

elbow grease – Hard work.

elephant's trunk – It is a rhyming slang meaning drunk.

elevenses – (1) A coffee break. (2) A light mid-morning tea.

Emerald City - It is a nickname for Sydney.

Emma Chisit? – How much it cost?

empties – The empty beer bottles.

Enzed – New Zealand.

esky – A portable cooler or icebox for food and drinks.

even stevens – Equal amount or equal chance.

evo – evening.

exxy – Expensive.

F

face fungus – (1) A beard of a man. (2) The hairs on the face of a man.

face like a dropped pie – Extremely ugly.

fair dinkum – It is an expression to assert that what has been said by someone is genuine.

fair enough – It is an expression to accept that what has been said by someone is acceptable or reasonable.

fair go – (1) An equal opportunity. (2) A fair or reasonable course of action. (3) Appeal for someone to show more fairness or be more reasonable.

fair shake of the sauce bottle – Be fair.

fairy bread – A sweet treat that is frequently served at children's parties in Australia, and it is made of white bread that is sliced, buttered and cut into triangles and sprinkled with tiny coloured sugar balls called hundreds and thousands.

fairy floss – Candy floss.

fang carpenter – A dentist.

Farmer Giles - It is a rhyming slang for piles meaning Haemorrhoids.

fat as a match – It is a person who is very thin.

fella – A bloke or a guy.

feral – (1) Dirty. (2) Disgusting. (3) Disobedient. (4) Uncontrollable.

fibber – A liar.

fiddlesticks – (1) False. (2) Nonsense.

fielder – A bookmaker.

firey – A firefighter.

first cab off the rank – To be the first one to take advantage of an opportunity.

fisho – A fishmonger.

fit as a Mallee bull – Very healthy and strong.

fizgig – A police informer.

fizzer – (1) Failure. (2) Fiasco.

flake out – To collapse either from exhaustion or intoxication.

flannie – It is a checkered flannelette shirt.

flash – (1) Showy. (2) Stylish.

flash as a rat with a gold tooth – (1) Dressed out. (2) Ostentatious.

flat chat – At full speed.

flat out like a lizard drinking – Really busy.

flicks – A cinema.

flog – (1) To hit somebody. (2) To steal.

flutter – Wager.

flyblown – Penniless.

flybog – Jam.

fly country – The desert landscapes of Australia.

flossy up - (1) Dress up. (2) Improve one's appearance. (3) Make oneself tidy.

footpath – A pedestrian walkway.

footy – (1) A football. (2) A game of football.

forgive and forget – It is a rhyming slang meaning a cigarette.

fossick – (1) Search. (2) Search for mineral deposits. (3) Search unmethodically and untidily through something.

Four-legged lottery – A horse race.

freebie – It is something that does not cost anything.

Freo - It is an abbreviation for Fremantle. Fremantle is a seaport near Perth in Western Australia.

freshie – A freshwater Crocodile.

frog and toad - It is a rhyming slang for road.

from go to whoa – From start to finish.

froth and bubble – It is a rhyming slang for trouble.

full as a boot – (1) Extremely full. (2) Very drunk.

full as a goog – (1) Extremely full. (2) Very drunk.

full as a state school – (1) Extremely full. (2) Very drunk.

full as a tick – (1) Extremely full. (2) Very drunk.

full belt – At top speed.

full of beans – Full of energy.

full of it – (1) Full of nonsense. (2) To talk gibberish.

full on – (1) Challenging. (2) Intense. (3) Serious.

fully – Completely.

funny farm – A mental institution.

furphy – (1) A lie. (2) A rumour.

G

galah – (1) A loud-mouthed and stupid person. (2) It is one of the Australian native bird, and a kind of cockatoo, with its back covering in grey and its front in pink colour.

galoot – A fool or a silly fellow.

galvo – Galvanised iron.

game as Ned Kelly – Very courageous.

gander – Have a look at something.

garbage guts – (1) Someone who eats plenty of food. (2) Someone who will eat any food.

garbo – (1) A garbage bin. (2) A garbage collector.

gargle – An alcoholic drink.

gas-bag – An incessant talker.

gasper – A cigarette.

gawk – Look at someone or something usually in a rude or stupid way.

gay and hearty – A rhyming slang for party.

G'day!– It is an abbreviation for good day! It is a casual, friendly and a typically Australian way of greeting someone.

gee up – (1) To cause excitement. (2) To stir something up.

geek - (1) A nerd. (2) An uncool person.

Georgie Moore - It is a rhyming slang for door.

German band - It is a rhyming slang for hand.

get a wiggle on – It is a way of telling someone to hurry up.

get cracking – Start something quickly and decisively.

get set – To bet.

get the drift – To understand.

gibber – (1) A boulder. (2) A desert.

ging – (1) A catapult. (2) A slingshot.

gin sling – It is a rhyming slang for ring.

ginger beer - It is a rhyming slang for ear.

ginger meggs – It is a rhyming slang for legs.

gink – A silly person.

ginormous – A blend of the words gigantic and enormous meaning something is incredibly huge.

give birth to a politician – To discharge faeces from the bowels.

give it a burl – Give it a try.

glad rags – Best clothes.

glassie – It is a person who is hired by a club, hotel and pub to remove and clean used glasses and to empty ashtrays.

go bananas – To go crazy.

go off like a frog in a sock – (1) It is used to describe someone acting eccentrically. (2) It is used to say that something is really good.

go troppo – To become crazy.

gob – Mouth.

gobful – A lengthy and angry reprimand.

gonna – Going to. *e.g.* *'I'm gonna see my mate this arvo!'*

good oil – (1) A good idea. (2) The truth. (3) Useful information.

good on ya! – (1) Good for you! (2) Well done!

goodo – Okay.

googie – An egg.

goon – It is a cheap wine that is sold in a cardboard box containing the wine enclosed in an airtight bag with a dispensing tap.

gotta – got to. *e.g.* '*I gotta to go now.*'

govie – A government-funded residence.

Green can – A can of Victoria Bitter beer.

greenie – It is a derogatory term for a conservationist or an environmental activist.

Gregory Peck – It is a rhyming slang for cheque.

grim and gory – It is a rhyming slang for story.

grog – (1) Alcohol. (2) Beer. (3) Spirits.

grommet – (1) An inexperienced surfer. (2) A young surfer.

grotty – (1) Dirty. (2) Poor quality.

grouse – (1) Excellent. (2) Terrific.

gully-raker – It is a thief who steals cattle that are wandering at large or are lost, or that are unbranded.

gum tree – The Eucalyptus.

gunyah – It is a small shelter made of branches and paperbark, that the Aboriginal Australians traditionally build to serve as a temporary dwelling.

gutless wonder – A coward.

gutzer – It is a plan that does not work out.

H

Had a few – Drunk.

hairy goat – A poor racehorse.

ham and eggs – It is a rhyming slang for leg.

Hang on a tick – Wait a minute.

Happy as a boxing kangaroo in fog – Miserable.

happy as a dog with two tails – Very happy.

happy as a pig in mud – Really happy.

happy as Larry – Very happy.*e.g.* *'When Tim finally got a cold can of VB after a day of hard yakka in the hot sun, he was **happy as Larry.**'*

happy little Vegemite – A contented or happy person.

hard yakka – Hard work, especially manual labour.

hasn't got all four paws on the mouse – Stupid.

hatter – A loner.

have a yarn – Have a chat or discussion with someone.

have tickets on oneself – To be excessively proud of oneself.

haven't got a brass razoo – Do not have any money.

heaps – A lot. *e.g.* *'There were **heaps** of surfies at the beach.'*

heart as big as phar lap – This kind of expression is used to describe someone who is very generous and loving too.

hen fruit – An egg.

Hen's night – (1) It is a party specially organised for a bride who will spend time with her friends just before her wedding day comes. (2) A girl's or women's' night out together.

hills hoist – A rotary clothesline.

hit the hay – Go to sleep.

hoe into – (1) To carry out a task with vigour. (2) To verbally abuse.

hoick – To clear the throat and spit.

hold your horses! – Hang on!

hols – Holidays.

holus-bolus – (1) Everything at once. (2) The total.

home and hosed – Finished doing something successfully.

hoof it – To travel on foot.

hoon – A hooligan.

hoop – A jockey.

hooroo – (1) Goodbye. (2) See you later.

hottie – A hot water bottle.

how're you going? – How are you?

Howzat? – How is that? It is a request for approval.

I

ice block – (1) Frozen lolly. (2) Lollypop. (3) Popsicle.

iceberger – It is a person who swims in the sea throughout all the seasons of the year.

idiot box – A television.

iffy – Suspicious.

I hope your chooks turn into emus and kick your dunny down! – It is a curse saying that I hope you will have bad luck.

I kid you not – I am telling you the truth.

in fine feather – Full of vitality and spirit.

in good nick – It is an expression to describe someone as being fit and healthy or in good shape and condition.

in two shakes – A very short time.

inked – Drunk.

J

Jack and Jill - It is a rhyming slang for bill.

jack of – To be fed up or tired of something.

jackaroo – It is a young man who works on a large or a huge cattle or sheep farm.

jaffa – It is a cricket slang to describe an excellent delivery of a ball in a game of cricket.

jaffle – A toasted sandwich with a sealed edge.

jake – (1) All right. *e.g.* *'Everything will be jake now.'* (2) A toilet.

jam tart - It is a rhyming slang for heart.

jarmies - Pyjamas.

jiffy - A short period.

jillaroo – It is a young woman who works on a large or a huge cattle or sheep farm.

jim-jams - Pyjamas.

Jimmy dancer - It is a rhyming slang for cancer.

Jimmy Grant - It is a rhyming slang for immigrant.

Jimmy Woodser - It is a person who drinks alone in a bar.

Joe Blake - It is a rhyming slang for snake.

Joe Bloggs – An imaginary average man.

joey – A baby kangaroo.

John Dory – It is a rhyming slang for story.

John Hop – It is a rhyming slang for cop.

journo - It is short for Journalist.

jumbuck – A sheep.

jumper – A cotton or woollen pullover.

Jumpy as a wallaby – Someone who is edgy or very nervous.

just quietly – Between you and me.

K

kafuffle – (1) An argument. (2) A commotion.

kanga - (1) It is short for Kangaroo. (2) Money.

Kanga bangers - Kangaroo Sausages.

Kangaroo land - Australia.

Kangaroos loose in the top paddock - Intellectually inadequate.

keep nit – (1) To be on the lookout during illegal activity. (2) To organise people to protect or watch a person or a place.

Keep out of the rain – To avoid trouble.

Keen as mustard – Extremely eager about something.

Kelly – (1) An axe. (2) A crow.

kelpie – It is an Australian sheepdog that is bred from the imported Scottish Collie dogs, and it has a smooth coat of variable colour and pricked ears.

Kembla Grange – It is a rhyming slang for change meaning loose change.

kero – It is short for kerosene.

kick – It is a pocket on the pair of pants or trousers.

kick in – Contribute money or giving something.

kick the bucket – Die.

kick the tin – Donate.

kiddies – Children.

kiddiewink – A young child.

kid-stakes – A child's play.

kindy – Kindergarten.

king – (1) An expert. (2) To punch someone very hard suddenly and without warning.

king pin – It is a leader of something.

kip – (1) A nap. (2) A short rest. (3) Stay somewhere temporarily.

kiwi – A New Zealander.

Kiwi Land – New Zealand.

Knackered – Exhausted.

knickers – Women's underwear.

Knock back - (1) To consume an alcoholic drink quickly. (2) To refuse or reject.

knock 'em down rains – A violent thunderstorm.

Knock it off! – (1) Stop it!. (2) That's enough!

knuckle sandwich – A punch in the mouth.

L

lackie band – An elastic band.

laid-back – (1).Informal. (2) Relaxed.

lairise – To dress or behave in a showy manner.

Lamington – It is an Aussie sponge cake coated in chocolate and sprinkled with fine desiccated coconut.

land of the long weekend – Australia.

laughing – It is a word to describe someone as being in a favourable or in a fortunate position.

laughing gear – Mouth.

lead foot – A person who has a habit of driving a motor vehicle too fast.

lead somebody up the garden path – It means that one is not telling somebody the facts.

ledge – A cool person.

legend – A cool person.

leggie – (1).A leg spin bowler. (2) A leg spin delivery.

legless – Extremely drunk.

lemon squash - It is a rhyming slang for wash.

like a rat up a drainpipe – With great speed.

like a stunned mullet – Feeling shocked or surprise.

lingo – (1).Jargon. (2) Language.

lippy – A lipstick.

liquid amber – Beer.

liquid laugh – Vomit.

littley – A young child.

local rag – Local newspaper.

local yokels – These are the inhabitants of a suburb , a town , or something similar.

lolly water – A sweet soft drink.

London to a brick on - Absolute certainty.

long drink of water – It is used to describe a person who is tall.

loo – A toilet.

looney bin – A mental institution.

loop the loop - It is a rhyming slang for soup.

lose the plot – (1) To describe a person who becomes befuddled or irrational. (2) To describe a person who no longer can act or do things efficiently. (3) To describe someone as no longer fully understand what is happening in a specific situation, task, etc.

lousy – (1) Not good. (2) Unwell.

lower than a snake's belly – It is an expression used to describe a person who is contemptible or unpleasant.

lunatic soup – An alcoholic drink.

lucky country – Australia.

lung lolly – A cigarette.

M

Maccas – Mcdonald's.

mad – (1) Exciting. (2) Very good.

mad as a cut snake – (1) Extremely crazy. (2) Furious. (3) Very upset.

mad as a meat axe – (1) Crazy. (2) Eccentric. (3) Furious.

mad Mick - It is a rhyming slang for a pick.

maggie – A Magpie.

make a crust – To earn a living.

make a proper galah of yourself – To make a fool of yourself.

make a quid – To earn a living.

malarky – A foolish talk.

man in white – An Australian Rules Football umpire.

Maoriland – New Zealand.

mate – (1) A male person. (2) Friend.

Matilda – It is a bundle of personal belongings carried by a bushman.

mazuma – money.

me – (1) Mine. (2) My. (3) Myself.

Melbournian – A person from Melbourne.

Mickey Mouse - A rhyming slang for grouse.

Milk bar – It is a corner shop that sells bread, milk, snacks, sweets, take-out food and other groceries.

milko – Milkman.

mince pies - It is a rhyming slang for eyes.

mingy - Stingy.

mix it – To fight violently.

moccas - It is an abbreviation for Moccasins.

molly the monk - A rhyming slang for drunk.

mollydook – A left-handed person.

moo juice – Milk.

moosh – Mouth.

mopey as a wet hen – Feeling depressed.

mott – To stare at or to watch.

mozzie – A mosquito.

mud map – It is a rough map drawn in the dirt or mud by outback travellers after rain.

mud pies - It is a rhyming slang for eyes.

muddie – A mud crab.

muso - It is an abbreviation for musician.

muster - A bringing together of livestock, usually sheep or cattle.

mystery bag - (1) A meat pie. (2) It is a rhyming slang for snag meaning a sausage.

myxo - Short for Myxomatosis, a disease that is introduced to Australia to control the rapid population growth of the rabbits .

N

nails and screws - A rhyming slang for News.

Nan – Grandmother.

nappy – A diaper.

narked – irritated.

nasty piece of work – A very unpleasant person.

Nellie Bligh – It is a rhyming slang for fly.

Nervous as a long-tailed cat in a roomful of rocking chairs – Very nervous.

Nervous as a mother roo in a room full of pickpockets – Very nervous.

Neville – (1) A geek. (2) An unpopular person.

Nick off! - Leave me alone!

nick out – To go out for a short time.

nicky woop! – Go away!

nightie – A nightdress.

ning-nong – A foolish person.

nipper – A junior lifesaver.

Noah's Ark – It is a rhyming slang for a shark. *e.g.* '*Look out for the Noah's Ark!*'

no Arthur Murrays – It is a rhyming slang for no worries.

no dramas! - It is an expression of confidence that everything will be fine.

no great shakes – Not very good.

no good to Gundy – No good at all.

no-hoper - It is someone who is considered by other people as a failure or a loser.

no picnic – It is a term for describing something that is either difficult or unpleasant.

no probs – It is short for no problems.

no sweat – It is an expression to say that something is neither difficult nor problematic.

No worries! - It is an expression of confidence that everything will be okay.

nong - An idiot or a silly person.

nosh-up – A big or satisfying meal.

noshery – (1).A café. (2) A restaurant.

not a sausage – Absolutely nothing.

not enough brains to give himself a headache -- A stupid person.

not bad – Good.

not much chop – Not very good.

not my bowl of rice – It is equivalent to saying that I don't like it or It is not my cup of tea.

not on your Nelly! - It is equivalent to saying absolutely not or no way.

not the full quid – It is an expression to say that somebody is slightly silly or stupid.

NSW – It is an acronym for New South Wales.

numbskull – A dull-witted person.

O

ocker – (1). An uncultivated Australian Male. (2) It is a typical Australian male with qualities such as good humour, helpfulness and resourcefulness.

off like a bride's nightie – To depart or leave very quickly.

Oi! – It is an exclamation for calling out someone for attention.

Old Ned – It is a rhyming slang for bed.

oldies – (1) Old people. (2) One's Parents.

on for young and old – It is an argument or a fight in which everyone is involved.

Onkaparinga – It is a rhyming slang for finger.

onkus – (1) Bad. (2) Broken. (3) Unacceptable. (4) Wrong.

on the beak – It is a rhyming slang for reek meaning smelly.

on the blink – It is used to describe something as not functioning properly.

on the bugle – Smelling very unpleasant.

on the Murray – It is a rhyming slang meaning on credit.

on the nose – Stinking.

on the trot – (1) Continuous activity. (2) One after the other.

on the turps – Drinking Alcohol, usually in large amounts.

oodles – A large quantity.

Op shop – It is short for Opportunity Shop. A charity shop is an example of an Op shop.

OS – It is short for Overseas.

Oscar Asche – It is a rhyming slang for cash.

Oxford scholar – It is a rhyming slang for dollar.

Oz – Australia.

Ozzie – Australian.

P

pack of galahs - It is a group of disliked people.

Paddo - It is short for Paddington.

paralytic – Extremely drunk.

parrot mouth – A talkative person.

pash - A session of deep or passionate kissing.

Pat Malone - It is a rhyming slang for Alone.

pav - It is short for a parlova.

pavement pizza - Vomit.

pearler – It is something that is outstanding.

pester – To annoy or bother someone.

piccy - It is short for picture.

pissed - (1) Angry. (2) Annoyed. (3) Drunk. (4) Fed up. (5) Unhappy.

plonk – A cheap or a poor-quality wine.

Pommie – An Englishman.

Pommyland - England.

porky pies - It is a rhyming slang for lies.

postie - (1) A postman. (2) A postwoman.

poultice - It is usually referred to a large sum of money concerning a debt.

pozzy – A position or a spot.

prang – It is a crash or an accident due to travelling on the different modes of transport.

preggers - It is short for Pregnant.

pressies - It is an abbreviation for presents.

PT – It is an acronym for public transport.

puffed – Out of breath.

punt – To bet or to gamble.

Push bike – A bicycle.

put a sock in it - It is an expression telling someone to stop talking.

Q

QLD - It is short for Queensland.

Quack – A doctor.

Queenslander - It is a person that lives in or is born in Queensland.

quick quid – It is a modest amount of money earned with little effort, usually by dishonest means.

quick snort – A quick drink.

R

rack off! – Get lost!

rainmaker – It is an Australian Rules football slang meaning a very high kick.

ranga – A nasty term for a red-haired person.

rapt – (1) Delighted. (2) Pleased.

razz – To tease.

reckon – (1) It means absolutely when used as an interjection. (2) Suppose. (3) Think.

reef and beef – It is a dinner that is consist of both seafood and meat.

reg grundies - A rhyming slang for underwear.

rego – It is short for registration of a car.

rellies – It is short for relatives.

ridgy-didge – (1) Genuine. (2) Original.

ripper – (1) Awesome. (2) Fantastic.

ripsnorter – It is said of something that is admirable, remarkable or wonderful.

righto! – Okay!

road train – A big interstate truck with many trailers.

rock up – To arrive.

rock and lurch - It is a rhyming slang meaning church. *e.g.* *'We'll see you at the rock and lurch '*

rollie – A hand-rolled cigarette.

ron – It is short for later on.

roo – It is short for kangaroo.

ropeable – (1) Angry. (2) Bad tempered.

rough as guts – (1) Uncouth. (2) Very rough.

rough end of the pineapple – (1) A difficult experience. (2) An unfair treatment.

rouse on – To berate.

rug up – Dress in warm clothing.

S

SA – It is an acronym for South Australia.

saltie - It is short for a saltwater crocodile.

Salvo – A member of the Salvation Army.

same diff – Almost the same thing.

sandgroper - A person from Western Australia.

sanger – Sandwich.

scads – A large quantity.

scarce as hen's teeth – (1) In short supply. (2) Very rare.

scone – A head.

scorcher – A scorching day.

scratchy – An instant lottery ticket.

scungy – Unpleasant.

servo - It is short for service station.

sheila – (1) A girl. (2) A girlfriend. (3) A woman.

She'll be right - Everything will be all right.

shicker - Drunk.

shiny bum - An office worker.

shirty - (1) Angry. (2) Aggressive. (3) Upset.

shivoo - (1) A drinking spree. (2) A party.

shonky - (1) Not good. (2) Suspicious. (3) Unreliable.

shook on - (1) Interested in something or someone. (2) In love with someone or something.

shrapnel - (1) Coins. (2) Small change.

shut eye – To sleep.

sickie – A sick day. It is time taken off from school or work due to feeling ill and is often a pretend sickness rather than an actual one.

silly as a two-bob watch - (1) Idiotic. (2) Stupid.

Silly season - Christmas holidays.

sink a few – To consume some beers.

sink the slipper – To kick someone down.

skerrick – A tiny or insufficient amount.

skint - (1) Penniless. (2) Poor.

skippy – A kangaroo.

skite - (1) Someone who shows off. (2) To brag.

smash and grab - It is a rhyming slang for cab.

smokes – Cigarettes.

smoko – It is any short break from work.

snag – A sausage.

snot - (1) Mucus. (2) To punch someone hard and violently.

soapie – A soap opera.

sook – A timid person.

sool – To incite.

sparky – An Electrician.

speed merchant – A fast driver.

spew – To vomit.

spill the beans – To reveal a secret.

spill a yarn – To tell a tall tale.

spit the dummy – To lose your temper.

spitting chips! – It is an interjection to indicate that someone is angry or frustrated.

springy – It is a wetsuit that covers the body to the elbows, knees, and neck.

spruiker – It is a person who calls out to attract attention.

squizz – (1) To have a quick look. (2) To look.

stack - (1) An accident or a crash. (2) To have an accident or to crash.

stacks – A lot.

station - (1) A cattle farm. (2) A sheep farm.

steak and kidney - It is a rhyming slang meaning Sydney.

sticky beak - It is a rhyming slang for peek.

stinko – Drunk.

stirrer – It is a person who causes trouble.

streak – A tall or a thin person.

strides – Trousers.

strine – Australian Slang.

stroppy – (1) To describe a person as being in a bad mood. (2) To describe a person as being hostile and aggressive to others. (3) To describe a person who complains. (4) To describe a person who tries show that he or she is better or more important than other people by acting rudely or obnoxiously towards them.

stubbie – A small and squat bottle of beer.

stubbie holder – A polystyrene insulated wrapper for a holding a stubbie and keeping the drink cold.

stuff up – To mishandle a situation.

stuffed – (1) Broken. (2) Tired. (3) Useless.

subbie - It is short for a subcontractor.

sunnies - It is short for sunglasses.

Sunshine State - Queensland.

surfie - A person who goes surfing.

suss – Suspicious.

suss out – To investigate.

swag – (1) The bag of a bush traveller or a tramp. (2) A large amount of something.

swagman – (1) A bush traveller. (2) A tramp.

sweat on – (1) To continually think or talk about something, especially something unpleasant. (2) To wait nervously.

swimmers – A swimming costume.

Sydney harbour - It is a rhyming slang for barber.

Sydney or the bush - It is either all or nothing.

T

Ta - It is an abbreviation for thank you.

take a piece out of – Scold someone severely

tall timber – It is Australian Rules Football slang for a very tall footballer.

tanked - Drunk.

TAS - It is an abbreviation for Tasmania.

Tassie - It is short for Tasmania.

Taswegian – A Tasmanian.

ta-ta – Goodbye.

technicolour yawn – Vomit.

tee up - To arrange or organise something.

telly – It is short for Television.

ten ounce sandwich – It is a lunch consisting of beer only.

Territorian – It is a person from the Northern Territory.

That's the shot! – It is an interjection of approval signifying that someone is doing something correctly.

That's the way the cookie crumbles – That is the way life is.

The never never – It is the vast and remote area of the outback in Australia.

things are crook in Tallarook – A bad or unpleasant situation.

thongs – The Backless rubber sandals.

thunder box – It is a toilet that is usually located outside.

tick – A short period of time.

ticker – Heart.

tickle the till – (1) An employee who thieves from the cash register. (2) To steal from either a business or somebody.

tides gone out – Your glass is not full.

tingle – A telephone call.

tinnie – A can of beer.

to have a bib and bub – To take a bath.

to see which way the cat jumps – To postpone on deciding what to do next until you have seen how things are developing.

toey – It is used to describe a person who is edgy or nervous.

togs – (1) Clothing. (2) Swimwear.

Too right! – Definitely.

top bloke – A good guy.

top drop – A good wine.

Top End – Northern Territory.

Top Ender – It is a person from Northern Territory.

tradie - It is short for a tradesperson.

tracky dacks – Sweatpants.

triantelope – A large huntsman spider.

trouble 'n' strife - It is a rhyming slang for wife.

truckie - It is short for a truck driver.

true blue - (1) Real Australian. (2) Genuine.

twit – A fool.

two-pot screamer – (1) It is a person who is affected considerably shortly after drinking alcohol. (2) It is a person who gets drunk after the consumption of very little alcohol.

tucker – Food.

tuck shop - (1) A cafeteria. (2) A canteen. (3) An eatery.

tucker-bag – Food bag.

tuckerbox – It is a lunch box.

turf off - (1) To expel. (2) To reject. (3) To throw out.

tyke – A small kid.

U

U-ee – A U-turn.

Ugg boots – These are the Australian sheepskin boots lined with fleece on the inside and are worn to keep warm in the cold weather.

Uluru - It is also known as Ayers Rock and is the second largest sandstone monolith in the world and situated in the arid red centre of Northern Territory. Uluru stands 348 metres above ground and had a circumference of roughly 9.4 kilometres, and can be seen from space because it is massive in size. It is renowned for the changing colour on the surface on the monolith at different times of the day and year and especially evident during dawn and sunset. The area surrounding this monolith is home to the plethora of springs, waterholes, rock caves and ancient paintings.

umpie - It is short for an umpire.

underdak – Underpants.

underground mutton – A rabbit.

undies - It is short for underpants.

Uni - It is short for university.

unco - (1) A clumsy person. (2) It is short for uncoordinated.

under the weather – Feeling unwell.

unit - (1) An apartment. (2) A flat.

unreal – Excellent.

up a gum tree - (1) Be in a state of confusion. (2) Is in a predicament.

up oneself – Have a high opinion of oneself.

up the duff – Pregnant.

up the pole - (1) Slightly crazy. (2) Wrong.

up the spout - (1) No-good. (2) Pregnant. (3) Ruined.

useful as a glass door on a dunny – It is a derogatory term to refer someone or something as useless.

useless as an ashtray on a motorbike – Absolutely useless.

Ute – A pick up truck.

V

Vandyke – An outside toilet.

VB - It is an acronym for Victoria Bitter. It is a brand of a beer that is popular in Australia.

Vee-dub – A Volkswagen motor vehicle.

Vegemite - It is a thick and dark coloured food spread made from leftover brewers' yeast extract with vegetables and spice additives. It is an iconic food that has a robust and unique salty flavour, loved by many Australians.

veg out – To relax in front of the television.

veggies - Vegetables.

vego - Vegetarian.

Venture Scout – A senior member of The Scout Association.

verbal diarrhoea – Talking gibberish.

VIC - It is an abbreviation for Victoria.

Vinnies - Saint Vincent de Paul is one of Australia's oldest charities.

vino - A cheap wine.

volcanoes - (1) Boils. (2) Pimples.

W

WA - It is an acronym for Western Australia.

WACA - It is an acronym for Western Australian Cricket Association.

waffle on – Talk excessively.

wag – To Truant.

Wake up Australia! – It is an interjection requesting somebody to stop daydreaming and pay attention.

Wallaby – A small kangaroo.

walloper – A police officer.

Wallaroo – It is an aboriginal name for a large black Kangaroo.

Wally – A foolish or a silly person.

Waltzing Matilda – (1) It is also known as the unofficial national anthem of Australia. (2) It means to travel on foot with one's belongings slung over one's back.

wear the green and gold – This expression means to represent Australia in an international sporting event. Green and gold are the national colours of the uniforms representing Australia and are worn by these athletes when participating in this event.

weatherboard – A wooden house.

well oiled – Drunk.

weekend warriors – Army Reserve personnel.

Westralia – Western Australia.

what do you do for a crust? – What do you do for a living?

what's the John Dory? – What is going on?

whinge – Complain persistently in an irritating way.

whinger – It is a person who often whinges.

whiteant – To criticise something in order to dissuade somebody from buying it.

wicked – (1) Cool. (2) Excellently. (3) Very good.

windy – (1) Being anxious or afraid that something unpleasant will happen. (2) Nervous.

within cooee – Not far away.

wonky – One feeling dazed and became unsteady on one's feet.

wooden pegs - It is a rhyming slang meaning legs.*e.g.* *'I could feel that my wooden pegs are tired after a long walk today.'*

woofers – Dogs.

woop woop – (1) It is a vast distance travelled in the outback. (2) It is a very isolated place. (3) It is an imaginary town.

woozy – (1) Feeling dizzy. (2) Feeling nauseated. (3) Feeling unwell. (4) Slightly drunk.

wrong in the head – (1).Crazy (2) Eccentric.

wuss – A timid person. This term is usually referred to a male.

X

XXXX - It is a favourite brand of Australian beer brewed by Queenslanders in Milton that is an inner suburb of Brisbane and is the shortened name of the brand Castlemaine XXXX.

Y

yabber – Talk too much.

yabbie – Any Australian freshwater crayfish.

yak – Chatter. *e.g. 'Please stop yakking!'*

yakka – Work. *e.g. 'That was hard yakka.'*

yarra – (1) A fool. (2) Mad.

Yank – An American.

Yankee shout – It is a social outing in which each person pays for themselves.

Yankeeland – America. *e.g. 'I am gonna fly to Yankeeland to see me mates.'*

yap – Talking constantly.

yellow canary – It is a sticker that is placed on the windscreen of a car by the police to deem the vehicle as being unroadworthy.

yike – (1) A brawl. (2) A dispute.

yikes! – It is a mild interjection of astonishment or concern.

yobbo – An unrefined person.

yodel – To vomit.

yonks – For a long period of time. *e.g. 'I haven't seen him for yonks.'*

yonnie – A stone that is used for throwing.

You der! – You idiot!

You little beauty! – It is an exclamation of joy and triumph.

You're a not wrong! – You are completely right.

young and frisky - A rhyming slang for Whiskey. *e.g.* *'I'd like a cup of young and frisky please.'*

youse – It is a plural form of "you", and used to refer to more than one person.

You bewdy! – It is an exclamation of joy and triumph.

yummo – (1) Beautiful. (2) Tasty.

Z

ziff - A beard.

zilch - (1) Nothing. (2) Zero.

zit - Pimple. *e.g.* *'I have a **zit** on my face.'*

zizz - A light or short sleep. *e.g.* *'It is time for a **zizz**.'*

zonked - Exhausted. *e.g.* *'I'm feeling **zonked** today after a long day of work.'*

Printed in Great Britain
by Amazon

48947885R10040